# A POLITICAL BESTIARY

# A POLITICAL BESTIARY

## VIABLE ALTERNATIVES, IMPRESSIVE MANDATES, and OTHER FABLES

EUGENE J. McCARTHY
JAMES J. KILPATRICK

illustrated by
JEFF MacNELLY

McGRAW-HILL BOOK COMPANY

New York   St. Louis   San Francisco
Düsseldorf   London   Mexico   Sydney   Toronto

**Book design by Stanley Drate.**

Copyright © 1978 by Op Ed Inc.
Illustrations copyright © 1978 by Jeff MacNelly.
All rights reserved.
Printed in the United States of America.
No part of this publication may be reproduced,
stored in a retrieval system, or transmitted
in any form or by any means, electronic, mechanical,
photocopying, recording, or otherwise, without the
prior written permission of the publisher.

34567890    DO  DO    7832109


**Library of Congress Cataloging in Publication Data**

McCarthy, Eugene J.    1916-
    A political bestiary.

    1.  Political satire, American.  I.  Kilpatrick,
James Jackson, 1920-      joint author.  II.  MacNelly,
Jeff.  III.  Title.
PN6231.P6M25    818'.5'407    78-16601
ISBN 0-07-044395-5

# CONTENTS

*Forward!*      *7*

**The Mandate**      *11*

**The Bloated Bureaucracy**      *14*

**The Untouchable Incumbent**      *16*

**The Viable Alternative**      *18*

**The Impasse**      *20*

**The Aura**      *22*

**Tight and Other Budgets**      *24*

**The Charisma**      *26*

**The Flexible Goal**      *28*

**The Mounting Crisis**      *30*

**The Gross National Product**      *32*

**The Credible Deterrent**      *34*

**The Emerging Equation**      *36*

**The Filibuster and The Dilatory Motion**      *38*

**The Running Gamut**      *40*

**The Broad-Based Constituency**      *42*

**The Gobbledegook**      *44*

The Staggering Deficit     *46*

The High-Level Advisor     *48*

The Economic Indicator     *50*

The Parameter     *52*

The Dilemma     *54*

The Loophole     *56*

The Gathering Momentum     *58*

The Consensus     *60*

The Reform     *62*

Inflation     *64*

The Pregnant Pause     *66*

The Last Priority     *68*

The Qualm     *70*

The Quandary     *72*

The Leaping Quantum     *74*

The Paradox, or Pair of Doxes     *76*

The Investigative Reporter     *78*

The Budgetary Shortfall     *80*

The Reliable Source     *82*

The Political Spectrum     *84*

The Syndrome     *86*

The Blind Trust     *88*

The Vanishing Milieu     *90*

# FORWARD!

This book was conceived one cold November night in the home of James J. Kilpatrick, located a few miles west of Scrabble, Virginia, on the eastern slopes of the Blue Ridge Mountains. Overhead all the stars of the Northern Hemisphere sparkled in splendid array. Inside this modest mountain cabin, a fire crackled and flamed on the kitchen hearth. Two freeloading collies, one old, one young, snoozed underfoot.

There came a knock at the cabin door. The two dogs, ever alert to danger, lifted their heads. Who could this stranger be? In a trice their unspoken question was unanswered. It was Eugene J. McCarthy, no stranger he. Mr. McCarthy plunged in from the cold and embraced his host. His host embraced Mr. McCarthy. Mr. McCarthy embraced the collies. The collies embraced Mr. McCarthy. The collies embraced each other. Then they all had a drink.

During the course of a pleasant evening, as the flames leaped up and the bourbon went down, the two aging naturalists spoke of the strange creatures they had seen in the thickets of politics and in the seas of language. They spoke of words, of the health of the English tongue, of the difficulty of communicating thought in a mindless time. Both scholars had spent many years in Washington—Mr. Kilpatrick in pursuit of news, Mr. McCarthy in quest of truth. The two goals are often confused.

A little before eleven o'clock, or a little after (it does not matter), Mr. McCarthy made an observation that, even for him, was unusually profound. Paraphrasing and improving on Alexander Pope, he remarked that "the proper study of mankind is animals." The collies rose unsteadily to their feet and applauded.

At once the two venerable sages put two and two together, adding a dash of bitters and a splash of plain water. Metaphors caromed about the kitchen. Images sprang to mind. Mr. Kilpatrick recalled the Budgetary Shortfall he had seen along the Potomac. Mr. McCarthy spoke fondly of Leaping Quantums. The list grew quickly: The Staggering Deficit, the Galloping Inflation, the Impressive Mandate.

As the hours passed, the fire subsided but determination rose. The two political veterinarians concluded that a proper Bestiary should no longer be withheld from the scientific community. Satisfied that their own prose efforts would improve understanding and communication, they recognized that words alone would not suffice. What was needed was something more. One for the road? No. What was needed was an artist of truly distinguished stature in the field of animal illustration. One name occurred to them both—the name of Jeff MacNelly, the Pulitzer Prize-winning cartoonist of the *Richmond* (Va.) *News Leader.* Shortly after dawn, or shortly before (it does not matter), Mr. MacNelly was routed from his slumbers by a reasonable request that he draw a Dilatory Motion.

This indispensable volume is the result.

# A POLITICAL BESTIARY

# THE MANDATE

Mandates come in as many varieties as finches, warblers, sparrows, and Southern politicians. They are generally divided into Greater Mandates and Lesser Mandates.

Among the Greater Mandates are the Impressive Mandate and the Overwhelming Mandate. The Lesser Mandates include the Slim Mandate, the Doubtful Mandate, and the Uncertain Mandate.

Greater Mandates usually are discovered almost immediately after elections, gamboling about the White House lawn. They appear like tree frogs in early March or old friends after a victory at the polls.

Lesser Mandates are more difficult to find, even though they come in many sizes and forms. Highly sensitive Presidents and other elected officeholders rarely perceive a Slim Mandate. Political columnists, however, regularly confirm valid sightings.

Some Mandates, of course, are more visible than others. And in certain circumstances, even a Greater Mandate may disappear altogether. In November 1972, it will be recalled, an Overwhelming Mandate was widely remarked. But by the early summer of 1974, this curious creature had become a Disappearing Mandate. By mid-August it was gone.

It is said by some students that a President of the United States, because of the special powers of his office, can create his own Mandate. The theory is groundless. Elected officials do not *win* a Mandate or *achieve* a Mandate, and they cannot possibly *create* a Mandate. The voters *give* them a Mandate or

# THE SLIM MANDATE

*present* them with a Mandate. These are the proper verbs. No other verbs may be accepted.

When a Mandate has been given, the Mandate must be acted upon. This is fine with the Mandate, for he knows he will not be acted upon for long.

It needs only to be added that the Mandate has no homing instinct. Unless carefully watched and cared for, he will wander away and never return.

# THE BLOATED BUREAUCRACY

Among the most familiar creatures of the political seas is the Bloated Bureaucracy. The species is almost always accompanied by its adjective. Mill in 1848 wrote of the Dominant Bureaucracy. A decade later, according to the OED, an unidentified writer spoke of the Brigand Bureaucracy of China. In our own time, we encounter the Entrenched Bureaucracy. But the preferred form, used by cultivated orators and writers everywhere, is Bloated Bureaucracy.

Bloat is no laughing matter; a bloated government has serious digestive problems. The more it eats, the more it wants; the more it wants, the more it eats.

The BB has a life span that ranges somewhere between the infinite and the eternal. This is partly owing to the languid nature of the species: the Bloated Bureaucracy cannot be hurried; it swims at its own pace. The BB's longevity also is attributed to the thick scales with which its body is armored. Through this protective covering the barbed shaft can seldom penetrate. Editors, Senators, taxpayers, Jimmy Carter—they have all had a crack at insulting the Bloated Bureaucracy. Nothing takes. The fossil remains of this durable creature have been carbon-dated from the tombs of the pharaohs and may be encountered in Washington and in the several state capitols to this very day.

# THE UNTOUCHABLE INCUMBENT

Incumbents were not always as untouchable as they are now. There was a time when Non-Incumbents were quite free to challenge Incumbents, to touch them, to wrestle with them, even (as it is said) to unseat them. But gradually Incumbents began to develop special protection. They evolved in the manner of the porcupine: They grew longer and longer quills. At the same time they passed laws limiting the length and sharpness of the quills of Non-Incumbents. This was known as election reform.

Incumbents developed the special protective idea of seniority. This marvelous principle asserts that the longer one holds a position, the stronger one's claim is to it. Thus the Untouchable Incumbent asserted his right to certain trees, those with the sweetest bark and the most advantageous limbs for climbing, leaving Non-Incumbents vulnerable to easy attack down below.

Today the Incumbents feed on the juiciest leaves high on the tree, their diet consisting principally of choice prerogatives, traditional perquisites, special privileges, and fringe benefits.

On such a rich diet, with their tree-parking places carefully reserved, Incumbents tend to build up heavy layers of fat just below their quill-protected skin. This comforting blubber is called a pension. It is this on which they live, in the event that they give up their Incumbency, or if because of carelessness or overweight they are dislodged or fall out of their trees. In this case a new Incumbent speedily picks up the ways of the old, enjoys the advantages of Incumbency, and usually finds in those advantages virtues that he had altogether failed to note before becoming an Incumbent himself.

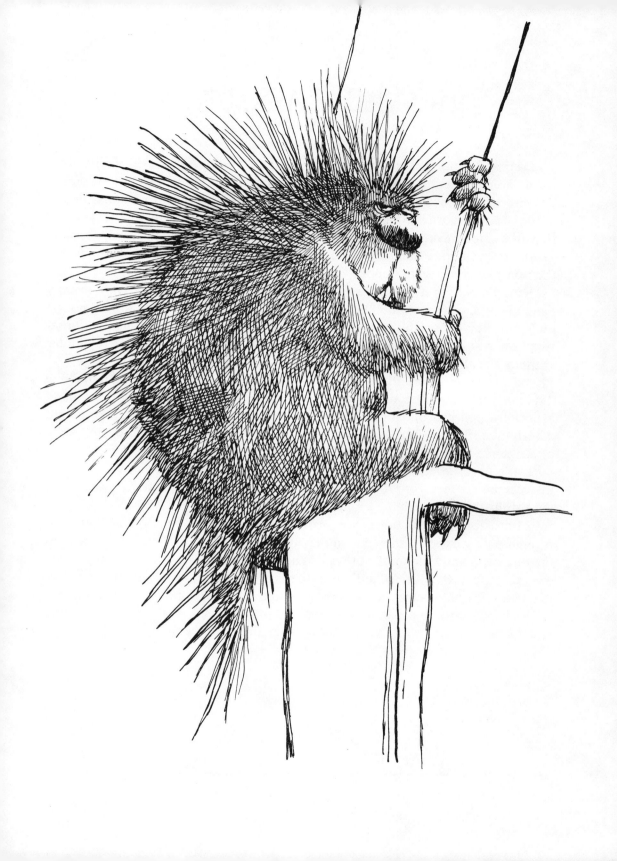

# THE VIABLE ALTERNATIVE

Distinguishing between the Viable and the Non-Viable Alternative is a formidable challenge even for experts. It is comparable to the test of distinguishing between the poisonous and non-poisonous mushroom. (Although failure to distinguish properly between the Viable and the Non-Viable Alternative does not have consequences of such immediate, evident, and absolute seriousness as does failure to distinguish properly between the poisonous and the non-poisonous mushroom.)

Non-Viable Alternatives, as a rule, are not difficult to find. They usually hang around, hoping to be noticed. They sit with arms folded and will not be budged. They tend to be stumbled over. Stumbling over a Non-Viable Alternative can result in great loss of time and may leave the Alternative hunter without a real Alternative.

Many Viable Alternatives are short-lived. An Alternative that is Viable one day may be dead the next day. On the other hand, a change in climate, especially political climate, may cause the revitalization of a dead or torpid Alternative. Some Alternatives have been known to revive after living in a state of suspended animation for years.

Little need be said of a third variety, the Unthinkable Alternative. The best that can be claimed for Unthinkable Alternatives is that they are regularly, but regretfully, thought about.

Alternative experts are distinguished by their language. Like lawyers and foreign policy experts, they say things such as "yes but" or "either/or" and "on the one hand and then on the other." When "Either/or" Alternatives meet, only one can survive. "Both/and" Alternatives, on the other hand, can live together—if not in harmony, at least within the tolerable range of adjustment.

Viable Alternatives, if not recognized and noticed, will often lie around making reproachful sounds and saying something that sounds like "I told you so."

# VIABLE and NON-VIABLE ALTERNATIVES

# THE IMPASSE

Although Impasses are found on all continents, the most serious Impasse, the most impassive, is to be found in the desert areas of Northern Africa and in the arid regions of the Middle East. For some reason not yet determined, Impasses appear to be moving out of their normal range.

At Helsinki in July 1975, experts thought they saw an Impasse near the hotel where the Americans were staying. It turned out to be only a cold moose. A second report of an Impasse in Damascus in 1977 was discounted when the Impasse disappeared before its presence could be confirmed by independent observers. *Newsweek* in April 1978 reported a fully verified Impasse in Bagdad. It hung around until summer.

Not much can be done to drive off an Impasse. Usually it will hold its position until the interloper who has come upon it goes away.

The best rule for dealing with Impasses is to avoid them or to circumvent them. In the case of the Bagdad Impasse, investigators found that there was no scarcity of food in the normal range of the Impasse. It is assumed that the Impasse came down to the city to get away from a stale mate in the desert.

# The AURA

The Aura was noted first in high places, marked by mystery (an Aura of mystery or a mysterious Aura), and associated with the divinities.

Later the Aura moved down to the range of heroes. Warriors began to show up with Auras of invincibility. So the Auras descended gradually from high places to the fields of battle, to the realms of religion and politics. Leaders in all of these fields sought Auras.

The Aura did not rest with these relatively lofty callings, but descended even farther. It became domesticated. New varieties of Auras showed up. The Aura of domesticity became common along with the Proletarian Aura and the Aura of the Common Man. When the common man made a mistake, it became known as Human Aura.

Television commentators are unusually keen observers of Auras. They can see an Aura coming from afar and can identify it quickly, in much the same way that they can spot a Momentum gathering, even in fog or rain.

Despite decline from the near-supernatural to the natural, from the ceremonial to the practical, Auras generally remain proud and of good spirit. Like the goat they remember their beginnings and hold their heads high.

# TIGHT AND OTHER BUDGETS

Budgets, grown more or less in the dark and fed with special nutrients, inflation additives, cost-plus vitamins, and normal accretions, rise from the murky waters of public finance in various forms. They are regularly identified by those who present them as lean and sober, generally as tight, sometimes as frugal and austere, often as bare-boned. They usually are seen by others as padded, bloated, and larded with fat.

Budgets may appear impregnable, but they live a perilous life. In the familiar life cycle, a Budget no sooner appears than cries are heard to "cut the Budget!" One then observes the cut across the board, the trimming away of fat, and the cut that goes to the bone.

Tight budgets are believed to suffer distress. Politicians, always sensitive to the discomfort of animals and the displeasure of the Humane Society, are especially sensitive to the discomfort of the Budget. Given half a chance, they will attempt to treat its discomfort with bromides, skin relaxers, sitz baths, and upward revisions of the revenue estimates.

Tight Budgets, with assistance, have been known to shed their skins as snakes do, or as some crabs shed their shells, thus relieving the pressure and making what appeared to be a Tight Budget a pleasantly loose one.

THE TIGHT BUDGET

# THE CHARISMA

The Charisma is closely related to the Aura, although it differs in several respects. The range of the Aura is wider than that of the Charisma. The Aura is less likely to attach itself to particular persons, although it sometimes does. More commonly it associates itself with larger movements of history, with events, or with group actions. The Charisma, however, is highly personal, like the one-person dog.

Until recently the Charisma attached itself only to persons of strong religious or mystical inclination. For some reason, possibly the decline of religion and mysticism and the rise of secularism, Charismas have become less discriminating. They have become secularized and identified with purposes far less elevated than their original commitments—or identified with no purposes at all.

Charismas can be cultivated—that is, raised in captivity. But the more common way to obtain one is to capture it in the wild (it most often is found among Charismas trees) and then to domesticate it.

Even a Charisma raised in captivity carries a strain of restlessness. If not properly nurtured and cared for it may revert to its natural state and leave the person to whom it was attached, much like the falcon.

When a Charisma vanishes, it leaves its owner destitute and at a loss to explain what has happened to his former powers. With Charisma in attendance, one can make mistakes of judgment without being challenged, commit immoral acts without being criticized, and generally act with freedom and panache. A person with the right Charisma can do almost anything.

# THE FLEXIBLE GOAL

The Flexible Goal was first identified by Joseph A. Califano, Jr., Secretary of Health, Education and Welfare, in the early spring of 1977. He was striding along the banks of the Potomac, deep in thought, pondering the distribution of Federal aid for higher education. Already acclaimed as a man of action, Mr. Califano wanted to be still better known as a man of affirmative action, but the path to that reputation was filled with potential pitfalls. His task was to fix certain numerical quotas without actually fixing the quotas numerically: a tough assignment.

Then suddenly he spied in the grass beside the river a friendly reptile, comfortably curled against a weeping willow. It was the Flexible Goal, a shapely and sinuous creature, dressed in jade green and carrying an abacus. Mr. Califano peered into the creature's melting eyes and saw that his problems were solved. For the Flexible Goal was his heart's desire.

This Goal is not a Goal, exactly. Neither is it a quota, precisely. The Flexible Goal feeds on specific percentages but it never gives birth to numbers, absolutely. A mature Flexible Goal asks only to be pursued in good faith; it is not to be captured, this year or next; it is only to be sought after or aspired to.

For the bureaucratic sportsman who abhors quotas, the Flexible Goal makes the perfect companion. It is capable of coiling, uncoiling, sliding, slipping, amending, revising, perpetually nearing—it defies definition. In the world of affirmative action (Mr. Califano's world), it is the symbol of rubbery rigidity, the sign of positive vagueness.

# THE MOUNTING CRISIS

It might be supposed, considering the nature of the beasts, that Crises are as rare as pileated woodpeckers. This was true in another era, but in our own century Crises have returned from the brink of extinction. Now Crises abound.

In 1978 alone, merely in the city of Washington, scores of Crises were sighted and recorded. Taking the first quarter as typical, one recalls that Mr. Carter was grappling with the Coal Crisis, the Dollar Crisis, the Mideast Crisis, the Energy Crisis, and a Crisis of Confidence—all at the same time. The President also was attempting to cope with a Crisis on the farms, a Crisis in the cities, and a Crisis in his relations with blacks, Congress, and the Jewish voters of Florida and New York. A Crisis was approaching, or so it was said, in his own political fortunes.

We have chosen to illustrate the Mounting Crisis, because this is the most familiar form. At some point in its life span, every Crisis mounts.

Experts are divided on the question of what becomes of the Mounting Crisis. Some authorities believe that Crises are resolved; some report that Crises fade. From our own observations we have concluded that Crises simply disappear. Sometimes they also reappear. One day they are all over page one; they dominate the evening news on TV. The next day one detects no mention of them. Then, after some lapse of time, they return, still mounting. A Sturdy Crisis, fed a balanced diet of facts and rumors, can keep this up indefinitely. Consider the Mideast Crisis. It has been mounting for four millennia.

# THE GROSS NATIONAL PRODUCT

Our domestic Gross National Product, in the eyes of other Gross National Products, doubtless is beautiful. In a less prejudiced view, the Gross National Product is not especially pleasant to look at. It is, to begin with, *gross.*

The GNP, as it is universally known, is a highly productive animal, and until recently it produced more than it consumed. Its equivalency measure, like the corn–hog ratio used in Iowa to compute the efficiency of pork production, was favorable.

In recent years, despite the efforts of fiscal veterinarians, the GNP has begun to consume more than its produces. Its handlers have had to import additional supplements, reflected in an unfavorable balance of trade and in Galloping Inflation. Its corn–hog ratio, as it were, no longer attracts admiration.

The Gross National Product eats almost anything, from hog bellies to soybeans. Its favorite drink is oil, both foreign and domestic. Because of this mixed diet, its tissues vary greatly in strength and firmness. Some are in prime condition, taut and lean; others are wasted and flabby.

Politicians are constantly trying, like body builders through diet and exercise, to redistribute the weight of the Gross National Product. They have had little luck. A few handlers, unable to turn flab into muscle, or to encourage or to entice the GNP to discipline itself, are advocating zero growth. This is no easy goal, because the whole metabolism of the animal in recent years has been conditioned to rapid if not to unlimited growth.

It now appears that, as with the dinosaurs, while the body grew large, the brain of the GNP remained small. Consequently its control over the body, especially the pedal extremities, has been less than fully efficient, to the point that some of the highly concentrated nerve centers are beginning to act independently of the central brain control. Experts are worried. What will happen, they ask themselves, when all the scattered nerve-cell centers become independent?

The hindquarters of the Gross National Product may then seek to go in one direction while the front is struggling to go in another, and its disposition to consume more than it produces will get completely out of hand. This is what happened to the Gross National Product in Germany in the period after World

War II. It munched upon binoculars, 35-millimeter cameras, and Wagnerian sopranos, and it produced Volkswagens.

This should be a lesson to us all. Never give a GNP too much to eat. It may feed next upon you.

# THE CREDIBLE DETERRENT

The Deterrent does not fit easily into any category of beasts. It is not a working animal. It is not a hunter, a watchdog, a guardian, or a defender. The theory behind its breeding runs counter to the traditionally accepted assertion that "the best defense is a strong offense." The principle bred into the Deterrent is that the best defense is a strong counterattack. The Deterrent does not know, or particularly care to know, what is coming. It does not need an advance warning. It will, it is believed, respond to any challenge. But such a response, necessary though it may be, marks a failure of theory. The theory is that anything or anyone, knowing that the Deterrent is waiting, will not come.

The Deterrent is still being improved. Breeders are working on two strains. One is the Credible Deterrent, about which there is a small measure of doubt: Will it really deter? Or merely defend? This type of Deterrent has been developed from the American Bison, whose strength is in its passive stand.

The other is the Incredible Deterrent. Its special power will be like that of the animal identified in some ancient Bestiaries as the Aurochs or Bonnacon. According to the medieval bestiary, this ancient animal was no threat, either offensively or defensively, from the front. But, the bestiary states:

However much of its front end does not defend this monster,
His belly end is amply sufficient.

For when he turns to run away he emits a gas with the content of his large
intestine which covers three acres.

And any tree that it reaches catches on fire.
Thus he drives away his pursuers.

# The Emerging Equation

Equations are aquatic animals. They feed on key factors, which are rather like plankton in political seas, and often they remain submerged for long periods of time. Indeed, Equations may remain undiscovered for decades or more, while Equation hunters, in the fashion of whalers, search them out. Like Captain Ahab, they are always looking for the right Equation.

It is believed by Equation hunters that if only the right Equation can be found, many good things will follow. There will be peace and justice. The lion will lie down with the lamb.

Columnist Joseph Kraft is one of the great Equation hunters of our time, especially for the Middle East Equation—which is very hard to find. Some Equation experts say that it is in the Persian Gulf; others say it is in the Red Sea or the Gulf of Aqaba, or in the Gulf of Aden, or even in the Suez Canal. Some students of early Equation history say that in fact it is submerged in the Dead Sea. Others say it moved to the Indian Ocean last August.

The search for the right Equation in the Middle East has been going on for roughly four thousand years. Occasionally diplomats have thought that the right Equation had been found, only to have it submerge. Several times an Equation, believed to be the right one, has been found beached on page one of *The New York Times,* only to have it turn out to be the wrong one after all.

Some cynics say that the search for a Middle Eastern Equation is futile, that it does not in fact exist. But hi, ho, and never say die. Even Walter Cronkite, a skeptical fellow, has expressed cautious optimism that the right Equation one day will be found in the Middle East. Since this significant expression of hope, Mr. Kraft and other Equation hunters have again taken to sea and have tentatively suggested that they have seen an Emerging Equation somewhere in the vasty deeps between Tel Aviv and Cairo.

# THE FILIBUSTER
# and THE DILATORY MOTION

The Senate wing of the U.S. Capitol ordinarily is thought about, when it is thought about at all, only in terms of the Senate chamber, the adjoining lobbies, the Vice President's office, and the visitors' galleries on the floor above. Not much is written or said of the dozens of little nooks and crannies and private offices where Senators go when they want to hide from their constituents or from other Senators. In one of these snug cubbyholes dwells the Filibuster, a beast whose talent is not to terrify but to bore. Sharing quarters with the Filibuster is his friend and constant companion, the Dilatory Motion.

The two of them seldom appear on the Senate floor. Often months will go by while the Filibuster and the Dilatory Motion snooze in their comfortable quarters. They eat old *Congressional Record*s; they read books that are both long and dull; sometimes they memorize bum poetry, famous orations, biblical quotations, and recipes for Southern gumbo.

But the day comes when suddenly they are summoned to action by the cry of a quorum call. Blinking his innocent eyes, the Dilatory Motion ambles to the floor and offers himself, with a litter of amendments, freely to be disposed of. At the end of a busy legislative day, the Dilatory Motion often is found upon the table.

Meanwhile, the Filibuster curls complacently at the feet of the Senators who have summoned his aid. His purpose is to get inoffensively in the way of all pending business.

Now and then the torpor is interrupted by spurts of activity. The Majority Leader sounds a blast upon his horn. Cloture! Then our drowsy subjects take to their heels with the agility of foxes pursued by hunters. But such activity rarely is observed. The normal pattern is for the pursuit to be called off and for the Filibuster and his furry companion to waddle back to their lair. There they hibernate, renewing their strength while they wait to be summoned anew.

# THe RUNNiNG GaMUT

Running the Gamut is thought to be an ancient pastime, not unlike the running of hares or of foxes, or even of possums and raccoons. Musicians were the first to run the Gamut, but they were followed quickly by actors, by politicians, and by sawdust preachers at Southern revivals.

It will be seen, however, that Gamuts differ from foxes, raccoons, and rabbits. These familiar creatures like to run and will run on their own, sometimes just for the fun of running. On the other hand, they do not like to be chased. At least it is not clear that they do.

Gamuts, on the contrary, will not run on their own. They have to be run, or chased. It is their function and their delight. Often Gamuts are run with little direction and purpose. Sometimes they are run like pointers and setters, quartering a field, through briars and brush. Sometimes they are run between two points. Dorothy Parker is supposed to have harpooned an actress who "ran the Gamut of emotions from A to B." In January 1978, President Carter in his State of the Union Message ran the Gamut of proposed Reforms from airline regulation to public welfare. That particular Gamut leaped over eighteen Reforms. It proved to be sixteen Reforms too many.

# The Broad-Based Constituency

A cow never voluntarily sits down. Because it has several stomachs, when it lies down it does so first with its front half and then with its rear half. The Broad-Based Constituency, on the contrary, never voluntarily stands up. Its strength and appeal lie in its broad base. Its movement consists principally in a slow pivot on its nether quarters.

Politicians constantly make the mistake of seeking Broad-Based Constituencies. The thought is that a BBC is reasonably stable and not likely to wander off, as narrow-based or narrow-hipped Constituencies often do. In time, however, Broad-Based Constituencies become a burden on their owners. As they become broader and broader their mobility decreases until in some cases they cannot move, even in search of food. They have to be fed incessantly.

Possessors of Broad-Based Constituencies frequently develop nervous habits. They worry whether the Constituency is happy, whether it needs water, or more food, or just reassurance. Often they will leave in the middle of a party just to run home and give the Constituency a few biscuits and kibbles and a glass of cold milk.

In consequence of its sedentary existence, the Broad-Based Constituency suffers from nerve and muscle deterioration in its lower back and demands to be regularly stroked or massaged. BBCs also become calloused and insensitive in their basic areas, developing an ailment comparable to bargeman's bottom, which is in turn comparable to housemaid's knee or barfly's elbow. It is very painful—so painful that it sometimes drives a Broad-Based Constituency to overcome its inertia and move, leaving the politician who has nurtured it bereft.

# THe GOBBLEDEGOOK

Of all the creatures catalogued in this Bestiary, none is more familiar, none more widely distributed in North America, than the Gobbledegook.

This lamentable beast has some of the characteristics of the common garden toad: He sits there, stolidly blinking, warts and all. He has some of the characteristics of the polecat and the inky squid, whose properties are to spread a foul diffusion. He has the gaudy tail of a peacock, the impenetrable hide of the armadillo, the windy inflatability of the blowfish.

It is commonly thought that the Gobbledegook resides only at seats of government, chiefly at the seat of national government, but this is not true. The Gobbledegook is equally at home in academic groves and in corporate mazes. He is often observed on military reservations, in doctors' offices, and in judicial chambers. He feeds on polysyllables, dangling participles, and ambivalent antecedents. He sleeps in subordinate clauses. The Gobbledegook is composed mostly of fatty tissues, watery mucus, and pale yellow blubber. The creature is practically boneless. Owing to cloudy vision, once he has launched into a sentence, he cannot see his way clear to the end.

In the foggy world of the Gobbledegook, a janitor becomes a material waste disposal engineer and a school bus in Texas a motorized attendance module. Here meaningful events impact; when they do not impact, they interact; sometimes they interface horizontally in structural implementation.

For all its clumsiness, the Gobbledegook is amazingly adept at avoiding capture. President Carter pursued his quarry through ten thousand pages of the *Federal Register* and emerged with no more than a couple of tail feathers plucked on the trail. The beast can survive for months on a jar of library paste; when startled by an angry editor, the Gobbledegook fakes a retreat, spouting syntactical effluvium as it goes, but once the editor's back is turned, the beast appears anew. It cannot be killed; it cannot even be gravely wounded. It dwells in thickets, in swamps, in heavy brush, in polluted waters, in the miasmic mists of intentional obfuscation.

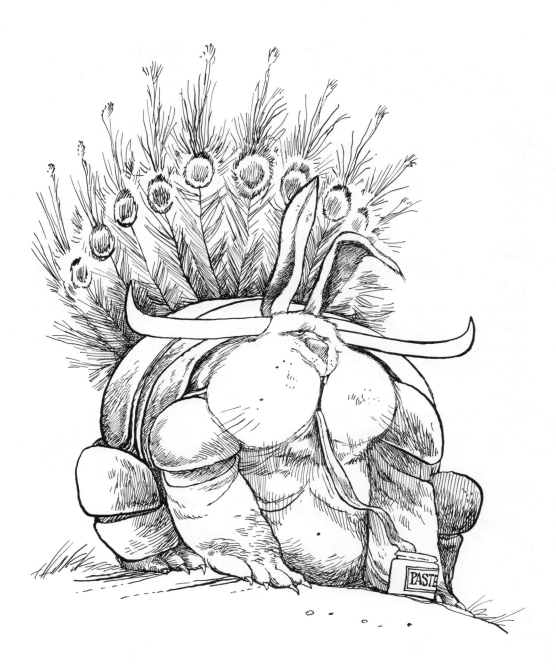

# THE STAGGERING DEFICIT

It is sometimes thought that nothing new ever emerges among the fish, fowl, and mammals that comprise a political Bestiary. But new species do come along now and then. One of the more interesting is the Deficit.

We have chosen to illustrate the Staggering Deficit, the breed most commonly found in the conservative press of the southeastern states. The *Macon* (Ga.) *News*, indeed, has never been known to record any variety but the Staggering Deficit. This is also true of the *Charleston News and Courier*, the *Greensboro News*, and the *Richmond News Leader*.

Yet it is one of the curious properties of this remarkable beast that the same Deficit known as a Staggering Deficit in Columbia, Savannah, and Jacksonville is known as the Not Intolerable Deficit in Los Angeles, New York, and Boston. One finds the Stimulative Deficit in *The New York Times,* the Modest Deficit in the *New Republic*, and the Acceptable Deficit in the *Washington Post.* These are all the same Deficits. Astounding!

From 1866 through 1893, no Deficits whatever were recorded. Some optimistic fellows thought Deficits had become extinct. Then Deficits began to be sighted again, and except for ten years of oblivion during the administrations of Harding, Coolidge, and Hoover, Deficits have been around ever since.

The Staggering Deficit came to prominence in the period after World War II, notably in the budgets of 1953 and 1959. After a memorably horrendous appearance in 1968, the Staggering Deficit became the Recurring Deficit. All Deficits have been classified as Recurring since 1970. It is expected that this condition will continue.

# THe HiGH·LeVeL ADVíSOR

High-Level Advisors are closely related to park pigeons. Both have a migratory instinct; they also have a homing instinct. They bow and coo a lot. They strut and waddle. They tilt their iridescent heads whenever a President speaks. They are by nature freeloaders. They move to and from the White House and other Executive office buildings. Sometimes they are driven out because of election results or because they have fallen into disfavor with a President, or with one of his principal aides. But usually after a decent waiting period they return to serve either the same President who sent them packing or one of his successors.

Some, driven from the White House, find refuge in academic cloisters. Some roost on the capitals of columns of well-established foundations, supported by money made in steel, oil, or automobiles. Others find a temporary home in established law firms, from which they sometimes make quick flights back to government agencies and financial institutions. Democrats tend to migrate during the off season to the Brookings Institution, Republicans to the American Enterprise Institute. These havens are like the Canadian marshes maintained by Ducks Unlimited—havens of breeding, incubation, and rest, where the High-Level Advisors can flock to strut, to waddle, and to wait.

HIGH-LEVEL ADVISORS

# THE ECONOMIC INDICATOR

Economic Indicators are much like the groundhog in function, excepting that they forecast economic trends and conditions rather than weather. Also, Economic Indicators appear to prophesy on the first of every month, whereas groundhogs appear only once a year, on February 2.

The Indicators are wards of the Federal Government. They are carefully guarded by the Joint Economic Committee of the House and of the Senate, which in turn is helped in its care and feeding of the Indicators by the President's Council of Economic Advisors. They are maintained much as were the sacred birds of the temple in ancient Greece, insulated from corrupting outside forces.

In all there are about forty-five Indicators housed in the official compound. Twenty of these are Major Indicators; the others are Minor Indicators or Supplemental Indicators. Among the Supplemental Indicators is the Deflator Indicator.

In their underground burrows the Indicators feed on root statistics and voluminous reports. They also eat developing trends. Indicators regularly give birth to Indices.

As the first day of the month approaches, the economic augurs, auspices, and haruspices gather to watch for the Indicators to appear. Among the famous augurs, auspices, and haruspices are Walter Heller, Milton Friedman, and Paul Samuelson.

Because some Indicators are treacherous and uncertain, and because some of them may not have fully digested their statistics or eaten their trends, expert analysis and interpretation are required. Moreover, because many Indicators are sensitive to weather, refusing in some cases to come out in the cold, interpretations must be seasonally adjusted.

ECONOMIC INDICATORS

# THE PARAMETER

To persons of limited horizons—those lacking the world view of, say, the editors of *Foreign Affairs Quarterly*—a Parameter may look like a perimeter. It is not.

A perimeter is orderly and manageable. It eats only dimensions. Even a nearsighted person can recognize a perimeter and anticipate its moves. A perimeter will go around its subjects. It has no place else to go.

The Parameter is for experts only. Novices should observe it, if at all, only by telescope and from a safe distance.

The principal food of the Parameter is perimeters. A Parameter also eats grant programs, statutory authority, and regulatory limits. If hungry it will eat an anti-trust prosecution, a welfare plan, a farm bill, or a Trade Regulation Rule of the Federal Trade Commission. The tentacles of a fully developed Parameter will embrace urban policy, medical care, auto safety, and the marketing of edible fruits and nuts.

In the world of politics, Parameters live to be defined. Their arms embrace the illimitable and the unknowable, but usually they embrace the expendable. "Within the Parameters of our budget," people say. Then the Parameter, like the squid, emits an inky cloud and disappears. This is why it is so very difficult to keep Parameters confined. They have a will of their own.

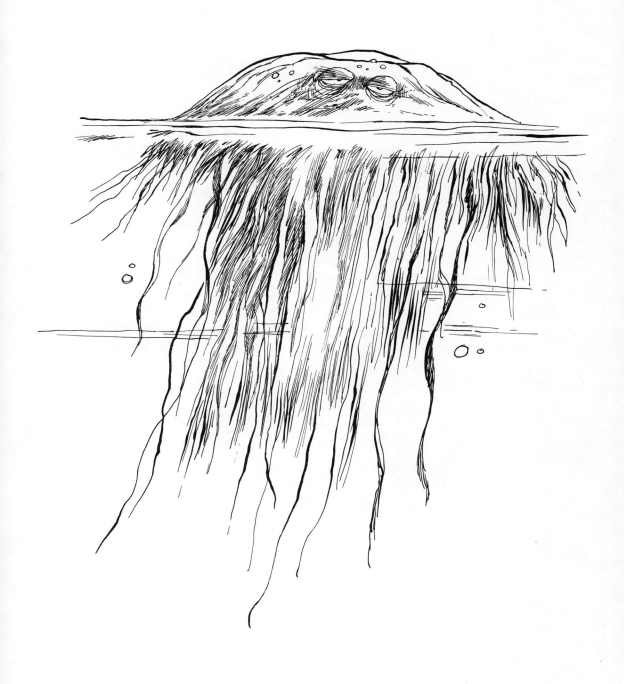

# THE DILEMMA

Three principal types of Lemmas have been identified. The Dilemma, or two-horned Lemma, is most common. The Trilemma, quite rare, is believed to reflect a recessive gene of the now extinct unicorn, which once must have broken its rule of celibacy to mate with a Dilemma. In a third class is the Hornless Lemma, either Polled or Dehorned.

The Common Dilemma is a distracted animal. Usually its right eye is directed at the tip of its right horn and its left eye at the tip of its left horn.

The horns of the Dilemma are particularly favored as trophies by debaters. A good debater usually has a rack or two of Dilemma horns mounted in his study as evidence of his victories over the subjects impaled thereon.

Lemmas sometimes are *found*, but more often they are *faced* or *confronted*. In such a situation, salvation lies in the Viable Alternative,[1] but in this fix, the Viable Alternative tends to get quickly impaled and ground under foot.

---

[1]Which see, *supra*, p. 18.

# THe LOOPHOLe

The first thing to understand about the Loophole is that it exists for one reason only: to be slipped through. This is all that a Loophole does.

A Loophole has this in common with Beauty, with Justice, and with a Fair Contract: It exists only in the eye of the beholder. For many years the most famous and familiar Loophole was the Oil Depletion Allowance. Those who were opposed to this provision of the Tax Code had no doubts or reservations: This was an Indefensible Loophole. But those in the petroleum industry had another view entirely. They saw the provision as reasonable, prudent, and wise.

The same skewed and simultaneous vision obtains in the matter of three-martini luncheons, Country Club dues, the maintenance of yachts and private airplanes, and the losses declared on the raising of beef cattle. One man's Loophole is another man's Sensible Clause.

The Loophole lives only within the subterranean shelters of the Tax Code. It swims in the dark waters of obscurity. Now and then it surfaces, gazes about with its bland and innocent eye, and then submerges before the random shots of the people who run Common Cause. The Loophole feeds exclusively, of course, upon the plankton of tax benefits. Its steel scales protect it from editorial attack. It lives almost forever. The Loophole is constantly assailed by poor demagogues and rich politicians but it seldom is destroyed. Properly domesticated, the Loophole makes a faithful and engaging pet. People who have their own Loopholes almost never let them go.

# THe GaTHeRING MOMeNTUM

The Momentum, before it has gathered, is a loose-jointed beast. It is as flexible and disjointed as a snake.

Until it has gathered, a Momentum is hard to identify. It may look like a Power Vacuum or a Developing Trend. Its spoor is often confused with the trail of an Emerging Consensus. The practiced eye, however, can detect a Momentum the moment it begins to gather. Like the slow pulling together of the furry caterpillar on its way to becoming a butterfly, the gathering of a Momentum is more subtle than the slow coiling of the snake.

Momentums will not gather unless conditions of temperature, humidity, air quality, altitude, habitat, and even barometric pressure are exactly right. The prediction of when a Momentum will gather, and the measure of its strength after it has gathered, are acts of science that are mastered only by a few political columnists. They alone can divine when a Momentum has gained impetus. Without impetus, Momentums are said to be faltering.

Amateurs and inexperienced observers should not take chances around Momentums. Once gathered, a Momentum can be held in check only for a very short time. Unless its wishes are granted, it is likely to break loose, like a hurricane, a flood, or a boozy orator, and sweep away everything in its path. Now and then, to be sure, a promising Momentum wilts overnight. The trouble, we are told, is that it peaked too soon.

# THE CONSENSUS

The Consensus is a problem to the natural scientists. It has no before. It has no after. It is a coming together not unlike the aardvark, which did not evolve from any other animal and is not evolving into any other. It follows that it is no easy job to generate a Consensus.

The Consensus also is like the Mandate. It can be compared to a Gathering Momentum that has not yet started to move. It has some of the attributes of the Aura. But no one of these—the Mandate, the Momentum, or the Aura—can fairly be said to be like a Consensus.

The Consensus is especially noted for its digestive system. It chews a cud and has three stomachs, but it eats only soft foods because it lacks a gizzard to handle hard facts. The Consensus has little structure and very few bones. Generally it is said of a Consensus only that it *appears to be*. Hence when it disintegrates it vanishes quite completely, leaving behind only a fine powder, or ash, which does not lend itself readily to postmortem (or to psychoanalysis either).

# The Reform

The Reform comes in various guises. The most familiar include the Needed Reform, the Imperative Reform, and the Too Long Delayed Reform. In every guise, however, Reforms share this common fate—their lives will be short and their permanent effects will be few.

Like the vipers described in ancient Bestiaries, Reforms and Reformers tend to be destroyed by their own progeny.

The Reform may be ostensibly respected, but is seldom truly loved. The Reform goes abroad like a parson who has just hit the Listerine jug, smelling faintly of piety and antisepsis. The Reform is diligent and persistent and almost always worse than the condition just Reformed.

Reforms may be found in widely varying terrains, from the humblest home to the most sophisticated corporation. Ordinarily, of course, they are encountered in governmental situations, where the power of law may be imposed in their behalf. Early in 1978, President Carter succeeded Ralph Nader as the most vigorous proponent of Reform in Washington.

In the usual course of events, Reforms are spawned by elections in which Reform candidates seek to displace the politicians in power. Mr. Dooley, the eminent Chicago bartender, knew all about this. "A rayformer," said Mr. Dooley, "thinks he was ilicted because he was a rayformer, whin th' truth iv th' matther is he was ilicted because no wan knew him."

As Mr. Dooley might also have observed, such election contests have a dual purpose. The first, as to the opposition, is to throw their rascals out. The second, closer home, is to throw our rascals in.

# INFLaTiON

Knowledgeable observers have positively identified only two species of this unloved but indestructible creature. These are Creeping Inflation and Galloping Inflation. Nothing has been found in between. Inflation never has been known to walk, or trot, or canter. When it gallops uphill in circles, it is known as Spiraling Inflation.

Usually Inflation creeps in its early, somewhat secret life. Sometimes an Inflation will creep throughout its life, but this is thought to be rare. Other times an Inflation will break into a gallop almost at the moment of its birth. It races across the country, leaping Indices as it goes. Its double-digit track cannot be mistaken for anything else.

Inflations usually are associated with the higher economic cultures, where both the creeping and the galloping varieties may be seen. In the process of moving a simple and backward country toward a more sophisticated economic state, Galloping Inflation appears almost an act of nature.

Inflation feeds largely on Staggering Deficits and Inconstant Dollars. After a full meal, Galloping Inflation can become Runaway Inflation.

DO NOT FEED THIS ANIMAL!

GALLOPING INFLATION

# THe PReGNANT PAUSe

Until quite recently very little was known about the Pregnant Pause or the pregnancy of Pauses. This lack of knowledge did not arise from lack of interest but from the difficulty of study.

First, the pregnancy of Pauses was hard to identify. Second, the pregnancy of Pauses was of such short duration that there was scarcely time for observation. Moreover, it seemed that most pausal pregnancies never went the full term, but almost immediately miscarried.

Students of Pregnant Pauses also were unable to distinguish between male Pauses and female Pauses and were therefore unable to study the mating habits of Pauses or to note the beginning of a pregnancy.

Much of the uncertainty about Pregnant Pauses has been cleared up as a result of the presidential debate of 1976 between then President Gerald Ford and Jimmy Carter. In the first debate of that campaign, students of the Pregnant Pause, together with some eighty million Americans, had the opportunity to observe a pausal pregnancy that lasted twenty-eight minutes. There has been no comparable pregnancy suspense since the world waited for Mrs. Dionne to bring forth the last of her quintuplets in 1934.

As a result of the study of this longest-lasting pausal pregnancy, it is now known that there are neither male nor female Pauses but that the pregnancies are parthenogenic. It is also known that no matter how long the pregnancy of the Pause may last, nothing will be born of it.

# The Last Priority

Priorities once existed in great numbers, sizes, and varieties. They ranged over great areas of the world. There were First Priorities, Rearranged Priorities, and Ordered Priorities. There were Pressing Priorities, Prior Priorities, Residual Priorities, and Last Year's Priorities.

Given such abundance, Priorities became a fad. Everyone had to have them as pets. Persons of high and low degree spent happy hours rearranging their Priorities. Because they are edible as food, tasting something like sweet and sour pork, in time they became scarce. Their fur was used as a mark of distinction. Gradually they moved toward extinction, like ostriches, passenger pigeons, buffalo and an honest martini.

Now only one Priority remains. This is the Last Priority, identified by President Carter. After it goes, there will be no more Priorities. Authorities are uncertain whether this last specimen will live longer if it is maintained in seclusion or if it is kept in a public place. Experts also question whether the Last Priority should be retired on half pay or used like a Low Priority until it dies.

Meanwhile, the Last Priority lives peacefully in a small corral near the White House Rose Garden, feeding on promises and asking only to be loved. President Carter watches it every day.

# THe QUALM

Qualms seldom are found alone. Usually they travel in a pack. Qualms are not aggressive but they sometimes are as difficult to drive off as they are to live with. They often appear when least expected and in surprising circumstances.

Whereas they are not threatening, they are disturbing. The presence of Qualms may discourage one from action or at least cause hesitation and provide an excuse for a delay.

Like Trepidations, Qualms will gather around the edge of a clearing or down at the far end of a bar. From such a distance, they cast accusing glances. Their eyes are large, dark, and unblinking. They give voice with a gentle, persistent bleat. Some people find the bleating of Qualms comforting; they regard their attraction for Qualms as a mark of character, in contrast to the professed serenity of persons who never have Qualms.

It has not been clearly determined why some persons have Qualms and others do not. Researchers are looking into the possibility that some physical quality may be responsible—as, for example, it is supposed that vegetarians never have lice, whereas meat-eaters, because of some physiological characteristic, sometimes have lice. Other scholars are investigating the hypothesis that Qualms may be explained in terms of some subtle relationship, such as that reported to occur on barges. Old bargemen say that in signing on a barge, a prudent deckhand will first look for cockroaches. If cockroaches are observed, the deckhand is advised to sign on, because—according to veteran rivermen—the presence of roaches is assurance that there will be no bedbugs on board.

A few breeders, having caught a pair of Qualms, have raised them in captivity. A most successful group in attracting Qualms and raising them are the Liberal Republicans. Liberal Republicans like Qualms because they can overcome them. Regular Republicans cannot tolerate Qualms.

QUALMS

# THe QUANDARY

The Horn of Africa has attracted much attention in recent years. It has become the object of the study and reflection of experts of all kinds. Students of ethnic origins are studying it; African scholars and world thinkers have noted it. There is speculation that in many ways what goes on in the Horn is related to what goes on in other parts of the world.

In the midst of this anthropological and political interest, one naturalist has noted a previously unobserved fact about the Horn. Although the flora and the fauna of the area have been quite thoroughly studied and catalogued, there have been no reports in the area of the presence of the Quandary. However, on March 11, 1978, the *Washington Post* reported that one had been identified—noting that there is a "Quandary in the Horn."

This is both surprising and disturbing. A Quandary, especially if it finds a mate and reproduces, could quickly upset the political and ecological balance of the area. Quandaries multiply rapidly. Their period of gestation is remarkably short.

The most interesting observation about the African Quandary, experts say, is that a linkage may be developing between the African and East European strains which may eventually produce a new breed called a Detente.

# THe LeaPING QUANTUM

The Quantum first was identified in the fields of mathematics and physics, where its jumps were measurable and irregular. Later it migrated into the range of political science. Now it dwells almost entirely in the world of foreign affairs, where its jumping is not only compulsive but also highly erratic.

This is the remarkable thing about the Quantum: It only leaps. Or if you prefer, jumps. This is all a Quantum is known to do. He does nothing else. He has no time for anything else.

This too should be noted: The Leaping Quantum comes from nowhere. He goes nowhere in particular, at least in the present, though frequently we hear of a Quantum Leap *into the future*. The Leaping Quantum was observed in the People's Republic of China when Mr. Nixon made his famous visit to Peking. Then it was said that China had made a Quantum Leap into the Twentieth Century. The Quantum Leap similarly was recorded in Spain following the death of Generalissimo Franco. Quantums recently have appeared in some numbers in Africa. They sometimes bound backward, as in India. Ordinarily, however, the motion is forward, upward, outward, and on to infinity.

When Quantums mate, they mate for life or two weeks, whichever is shorter. Because of their incessant bounding around, they make poor pets but they make excellent tight ends.

# THE PARADOX, OR PAIR OF DOXES

Experts disagree on the correct spelling of these feline creatures. One school holds that it is proper to say or to write simply *Paradox* when one means a pair of Doxes. Another school says that *Paradoxen* should be preferred. The third, to which the authors of this work conform, uses the better-established *Pair of Doxes.*

The common, or Ortho, Dox is never a threat by itself, nor is it disturbing. A Pair of Doxes is something else. Doxes always travel in pairs and threaten from two sides, unless they are old and have been around a long time, in which case they are merely distracting.

Unless a person has exceptional peripheral vision, it is very difficult to keep a Pair of Doxes within one's sight. They seem to have an instinct for staying just at the edge of one's range of vision. There they sit, licking their paws, heads tilted, as objects of skepticism, public comment, and awe.

The Paradox never has been successfully domesticated. A Pair of Doxes cannot be made to work together. They are forever raising their heads, asking questions, showing off. They go their own way. And because of their disposition to remain at a distance from each other, their mating is something of a mystery. Doxes frequently are seen in the same terrain with the Leaping Quantum, the Quandary, the Qualm, and the Dilemma.

A PAIR of DOXES

# THe INVeSTiGATiVe RePORTeR

As a consequence of recent mutations, Reporters now appear to be fairly well standardized into three specialized breeds:

- Those that work primarily on scent, like foxhounds, are said to have a nose for news.
- Those that rely largely on sight, keeping their object in view, like greyhounds, are said to have an eye for news.
- A lesser breed, nearsighted and with little or no olfactory power, depending chiefly upon its hearing, is said to have an ear for news. They often become gossip columnists.

Investigative Reporters combine special gifts of all three breeds. They have amazing sight, like that of a hawk in the daylight and that of an owl at night. At incredible distances they can spot a smoking pistol, a dumb blonde, or a fat movie contract.

Their sense of smell is more sensitive than that of the truffle pig. The Investigative Reporter knows a truffle anywhere. He smells truffles from afar, in the same way that he can smell a publisher's advance.

The Investigative Reporter has a sense of hearing more subtle than that of the iguanas, the desert wasps, or the lizards of the Transkei.

The true Investigative Reporter should be judged by his or her fidelity to the pattern of the Dung Beetle, his entomological model.

The Dung Beetle follows cows. Some authorities believe it even anticipates droppings. Seizing upon the cowflop with its powerful pincers, the Dung Beetle rolls up small balls of dung and transports them to a hole the beetle has dug in the ground. The beetle places the balls into the hole, then lays eggs on the balls. The eggs hatch and the larvae feed on the dung balls.

The lesson of this entomological phenomenon should not be lost upon the perceptive reader: You can get a lot of mileage from a cowflop, if you try.

# The Budgetary Shortfall

Among all the species known to political ornithology, perhaps none is more familiar than the Budgetary Shortfall. This ubiquitous fellow nests wherever legislative bodies meet. You will find him in county courthouses, in city halls, in state capitals, and of course on Capitol Hill in Washington. Red-eyed, red-crowned, and red-breasted, the Budgetary Shortfall cannot be mistaken for anything else.

In Washington, Budgetary Shortfalls ordinarily are conceived in October, at the beginning of the Federal fiscal year. They emerge as fledglings just after the April 15 tax collections. By August they are full-grown, but they are peculiar in this regard: As they become fully fledged, their ability to fly diminishes.

The Shortfall may be identified by his peculiar cry, which is an off-key *Uh-oh! Uh-oh! Uh-oh!* It is the sound the Orkin man makes when he sees a termite. It is rather more pensive than the "uh-oh" voiced by South when the trumps break badly.

There are many Shortfall watchers, but in recent years the Assistant Secretary of the Treasury has ranked as the preeminent member and permanent chairman of the Society of the Budgetary Shortfall (SOBS). His function, on observing the decline in monthly receipts that presages the impending arrival, is to station himself at a window overlooking the east wing of the White House. When he is certain of his facts, he is required to fling open the window and to shout at the top of his lungs, "Mr. President! Mr. President! I have sighted a Shortfall! I have sighted a Shortfall!" Then he closes the window. This is all the Assistant Secretary does.

Budgetary Shortfalls are not well regarded in the political community. Like starlings, grackles, pigeons, and cowbirds, they are publicly denounced. When Shortfalls appear in significant numbers budget directors are filled with chagrin. The Senate waxes wroth. Now and then appropriations have to be slashed.

Meanwhile the Shortfall goes on its awkward and embarrassing way, never running, always on the edge of flight but always falling short.

# THe ReLiaBLe SOURCe

Reliable Sources sometimes are found within the criminal underground patrolled by officers of the law. In their more familiar coloration, however, they inhabit the fertile fields of journalism. Here they are quickly domesticated and become as tame as house pets; they require only an occasional feeding of flattery, plus the warm milk of public quotation.

Washington reporters have classified several breeds worthy of particular mention. Among these are the White House Spokesman, the White House Source, and the Senior State Department Official.

Reliable Sources seldom can be precisely described. This is because a truly Reliable Source seldom is seen at all. Often their existence can only be inferred from the tracks one perceives on page one in the morning. It is known that Reliable Sources generally inhabit shallow caves and shadowy places; they feed principally upon rumors fortified with a cup of classified facts; they speak from the side of one of their several mouths. They lurk.

Now and then what is thought to be a Reliable Source proves to be a Bum Tipster instead, but this sort of thing is rarely observed. Far more often, the Reliable Source proves to be completely accurate, for the Reliable Source is himself the source of the Reliable Source. During the delightful years of Henry Kissinger at State, senior reporters had no problem in analyzing the concerns of the Secretary; they talked with an Unimpeachable Source, and when the conversation with the Unimpeachable Source had ended, they said "Thank you, Henry" and departed.

# THE POLITICAL SPECTRUM

The Political Spectrum is distinguished from other Spectrums in that its range of color is more limited and its shadings are less subtle.

So far as the naked eye can determine, it begins on the left with ordinary barn red. In this coloration, the Spectrum is considered to be more dangerous than in its next color stage, a pink of two shades (old red and venerable pink) and one tint (parlor pinko).

In subsequent stages, on toward the right, color changes are accompanied by spasmodic body reactions called kneejerks. These were first identified by William White, one of the nation's greatest Political Spectrum watchers, in the 1950s.

The shades and tints of pink may be followed by a sick-green range, usually identified with liberal Democrats. This delicate hue yields in turn to a blinking confusion. It is what the chameleon endures when he traverses a square yard of the Stewart tartan. Here one finds a rapid change in political colorations of no commitment, from the baby blue of liberal Republicans to conservative grays and Old Navy blues, sometimes with a pin stripe running through them. At the far right we encounter the charcoal black reactionary.

Spectrum watchers who are interested in pursuing a serious study should consult the ratings maintained on the Congress by such organizations as the AFL–CIO, Americans for Democratic Action, and the American Conservative Union. You may then color the various Members of Congress accordingly, from red to royal purple to black.

# THe SYNDROMe

Syndromes are like mice and cockroaches. They are able to live in any environment habitable by man—below sea level or at high altitudes, in arid land or in moist and rainy areas, in cold or heat, on space ships or on New York City buses.

Some Syndromes are distinguished by moods: the Optimistic Syndrome and the Pessimistic Syndrome. Others are distinguished by the place in which they are found. Two Syndromes have been noted in the White House—the Oval Office Syndrome, which seems to survive changes of administration, and the Situation Room Syndrome, which President Carter brought with him from his submarine service.

Whereas the Oval Office Syndrome is reasonably quiet and unexcitable, the Situation Room Syndrome is noisy and hyperactive, although not as agitated as the Crisis Syndrome, which is not unknown to the White House.

The Syndrome is a relatively simple animal. If broken up it is likely to regenerate quickly into another Syndrome. Thus a quiet Oval Office Syndrome can become a Situation Room Syndrome, and even a Crisis Syndrome.

Both hard-shelled and soft-shelled Syndromes have been identified. These interesting crustaceans are like alligators: They have brains that are smaller than their cranial cavities. Thus, if a Syndrome becomes overbearing, the best thing to do is to flip it on its back, causing the brain to strike the top of the cranial cavity, knocking out the Syndrome. While the Syndrome is temporarily unconscious, the person being victimized by it can either escape or look for a friendlier Syndrome.

OPTIMISTIC SYNDROME

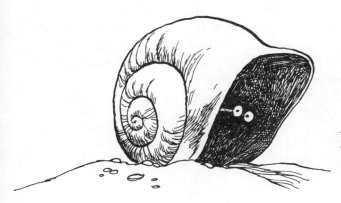

PESSIMISTIC SYNDROME

# THe BLiND TRUST

Before the true Blind Trust was developed, scholars had classified several Trusts of limited vision, some with impaired sight, some that were one-eyed, and some that were indifferent to what was going on. All these creatures, whose common charge is to guard the dear old nest egg, were exploited to some extent.

Over the years a greater social need for nest-egg tending developed. The demand for half-blind and poor-seeing birds—birds that could be trusted with nest eggs—outran the supply. Moreover, there was a suspicion that half-blind or indifferent Trust birds might show favoritism toward the nest eggs of birds who took up public-interest duties. Gradually the need arose for a fully Blind Trust. Once the need was recognized, the Blind Trust was quickly developed.

In appearance and method, the Blind Trust is a combination of penguin and chicken. Its large, webbed feet are equipped to protect the nest eggs until the parent bird, having fulfilled its public duties, returns to claim its nest eggs (or its young if the eggs have hatched).

It is popularly believed that the Blind Trust does not do much to advance the incubation process, but that it keeps the egg in just about the condition it was in when delivered. Some people doubt this. They also doubt that the Blind Trust always keeps the parent of the nest egg from seeing the egg during the period of trust. They suspect that the Blind Trust sometimes listens to the parent and takes advice from the parent as to the turning of the egg, the temperature at which it is to be maintained, or the possible exchange, scrambling, or poaching of eggs. There is also some suspicion that not all Blind Trusts are wholly blind, although they all wear dark glasses. A few skeptical scholars believe Blind Trusts can see in the dark.

Reform-minded egg watchers, led by Common Cause, recommend a Trust that is not only blind but also deaf.

# THE VANISHING MILIEU

No one has ever seen a Milieu from the front. Milieus are usually observed as passing or vanishing. The fault is not with the Milieu but with the Milieu watchers, who become so preoccupied with the Passing Milieus or with the Vanishing Milieu that they fail to see a Milieu approaching. By the time the Milieu is recognized it is too late to look at its front end. This is true of all kinds of Milieus—Economic Milieus, Cultural Milieus, Romantic Milieus, and others.

There are two schools of thought about the frontal characteristics of the Milieu. One school holds that the Milieu is cold-blooded and carries its head low (so as not to be observed as it approaches), and the other says that the Milieu is warm-blooded and has a long neck that it carries high, so that it can see whether the previous Milieu has gone or is going.

# ABOUT THE AUTHORS

Eugene J. McCarthy is widely known for a political career that has included several Presidential challenges, but better known for his treatises on the metaphysics of baseball. Among his lesser-known writings are a book of poetry, *Other Things and the Aardvark,* and a book of stories for children and Certified Public Accountants, *Mr. Raccoon and His Friends.* In the lull following his third-place finish in the 1976 Presidental race, Mr. McCarthy moved to Rappahannock County, Virginia. There, by accidents of geography and history, and by common effort sometimes called "collaboration," this book was written.

When he is not writing his syndicated column for the *Washington Star* or propounding his conservative views on CBS's "60 Minutes," James J. Kilpatrick husbands a varied livestock of three chipmunks, fifty groundhogs, and a flock of barn swallows on his farm in the Blue Ridge Mountains. His philosophical ruminations on the flora, fauna, and folkways of the region have been collected in a recent volume called *The Foxes' Union: Reminiscences of Happy Years in Scrabble, Virginia.* He is married and the father of two collies.

Like a latter-day Audubon, Jeff MacNelly has sketched and catalogued most of the major species of politico-vertebrates east of the Rockies and is currently on the trail of an exotic subspecies of California known for its ascetic habits and spartan habitat. MacNelly's credentials in ornithology are well established through his syndicated cartoon, "Shoe," and he keeps his pen on the pulse of the bureaucracy through his editorial cartoons. He can usually be found behind his drawing board at the *Richmond* (Va.) *News Leader.*